COLNE GIANTS

Tales From The Forgotten World of Knur and Spell

By
Paul Breeze
&
Stuart Greenfield

COLNE GIANTS

Tales From The Forgotten World of Knur And Spell

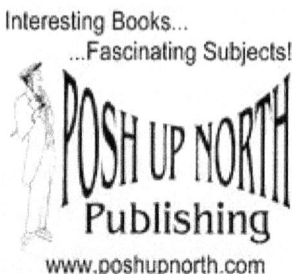

Interesting Books...
...Fascinating Subjects!

POSH UP NORTH
Publishing
www.poshupnorth.com

First published in Great Britain in June 2002 by
Posh Up North Publishing
Nelson, Lancashire

Reprinted 2018

© Paul Breeze and Stuart Greenfield 2002

ISBN 10: 0-9539782-3-0
ISBN 13: 9780953978236

British Library cataloguing-in-publication data.
A catalogue record for this book is available
from the British Library

Front Cover: left to right, Stuart Greenfield and Leonard Kershaw
Back Cover: Emmott Arms Handicap final, March 1958.

Tales From The Forgotten World of Knur And Spell

Stuart Greenfield
World Knur & Spell Champion 1970 and 1973

"Not many people on this planet get to become a world champion" -
Jack Charlton, 1966

Acknowledgements

We would like to thank everybody who contributed to the production of this book.

Everybody named below has played some part, whether it be providing background information, photos, funny stories, newspaper cuttings, taking us on trust and ordered a book prior to publication or purely carrying on the great tradition of supporting local sport with the whole family.

Geoff Crambie	Craig Walton and Chris Walton
Freddie Trueman	Jimmy Young
Neville Blackburn	Bobby Little
Michael Lee	Richard Wildman
Len Shuttleworth	Dave Whitham
Walter Ansell	Mary Maher
Ronald Ansell	Peter Copestake
Leonard Kershaw	Barry Smith
Shirley Bateson	Ernest Shepherd
Herbert Hipgrave	Frank Mottram
Hilda Jagger	Ernest Lowe
Donald Speak	Norman Gamson
Colin Madden	Tommy Mason
Mike Chapel	Ronnie Bolton
Joe Heap	Billy Walton.
Nelson Leader	Pendle Heritage Centre
Daily Mail	Lancashire Evening Telegraph
Yorkshire Post	Lancashire Library Service
W. Riding News Service	John Marshall Photography Ltd

Apologies if we have left anybody out, or spelt anyone's name incorrectly. Don't worry – we can just get our heads together and come up with another book!

CONTENTS

FOREWORD

by Geoff R Crambie,
September 2002

As a born Colner, I was proud indeed when Paul Breeze, a most respected author, asked if I would write the foreword to his latest book – Colne Giants.

My first encounter with the knur and spell came in 1951 when my dear mum took me to Colne to have a new pair of clog irons fitted. Being a typical 9 year old boy growing up during the post war years, one of my greatest pleasures (besides conkering and climbing gas lamps) was making sparks on the stone flags outside our house in Hall Street - especially when it was getting dark. However, this activity did take its toll on my clog irons

Sam Ansell was bonnie Colne's very last clogger of them all and Sam's shop had a true Dickensian aura about it with its ancient bay window and inside nooks and crannies full of boots, shoes and clogs. The window display was reminiscent of the "Old Curiosity Shop" and, among the clog irons and the leather bootlaces, was an enormous framed picture of Sam and his wartime colleague, Jimmy Young.

There was also a pile of strange white marble-type balls. My mum didn't know what they were so I went home and asked my dad. He broke off from feeding the 500 cage birds which shared our home to tell me: "Geoffrey, they are not marbles but pot knurs which are hit a very long way with a big stick in game called knur and spell." and that was my introduction to the great sport of tipping.

In later years, Sam Ansell and his brother Fred would become great friends of mine and I'm most proud to also know our town's two world champions – Stuart Greenfield and Len Kershaw.

The Knur and spell world championships of the early 1970s with Stuart and Len becoming champions and Sam as official referee was a time of great pride for our ancient market town of Colne and I'm certain that this book which tells of those halcyon days will be a proud possession of many a Colner.

INTRODUCTION

"My first experience of Knur & Spell would have been during the war when I was about 6 or 7. My dad took me to watch a game between his home guard colleague Herbert Bateson and the landlord of the Sun Inn at Trawden.

Completely unconcerned with the game itself, I wandered off quite happily to play playing in a bubbling stream down the hill when I suddenly heard a loud roar. I looked up to see a crowd of twenty or so men come hurtling down the hill towards me in a state of great excitement.

When they reached where I was playing, they were all asking me if I'd "seen it land...", meaning the struck knur but, needless to say, I hadn't a clue what they were on about.

Little did I know at that time that twenty years later, I myself, would be charging down the hill in a similar state of excitement on the way to becoming a world champion...!"

Stuart Greenfield, May 2002

**Knur and spell being played in the Yorkshire moors
in the early 1800s**
(Image taken from "The Costume of Yorkshire" by George Walker, first published in 1814)

Chapter 1: HISTORICAL BACKGROUND

Knur and spell has been played in the north of England for many years. There are numerous mentions of the game being played on the Yorkshire / Lancashire border in the early part of the 19th century and it is widely accepted that the game easily dates back to the 1400s.

However, the actual name is derived from words of foreign origin – knur coming from the Germanic word "*knorr*" meaning knot of wood and spell derived from the old norse word "*spill*", ie a game. This would suggest that there is more than passing likelihood that the origins of the game in this country may even date back further still – to the time of the Viking invasions.

Further strength is given to this argument when you consider that the game is only played in the north of the country, which is the region where the Vikings settled.

Tales From The Forgotten World of Knur And Spell

Another indication of this comes with the colloquial term for a knur and spell player – a "laker" (also referred to as a "tipper"). The verb "to lake" is a northern term meaning to play or perform, with regional variations such as "leyk" (West Yorks) and "layke" (Colne and Burnley). The origin of this word can be found in the Norwegian verb to play or perform which is "leike".

Add to that the fact that the Norwegian word for a stick of wood is a "pinne" – not unlike the "pin" that is used to support the knur in Lancashire – and the game's Nordic origins look even more certain.

There are various different versions and names used in different areas of Northern England. In his Encyclopaedia of Sports, John Arlott, commented as follows:

"It has affinities with trapball, dag and trigger (East Riding of Yorkshire) buck and stick, tipcat, billet, and nipsy – played exclusively in the Barnsley area where the sticks are pared down pickaxe handles and heads made from mangle rollers.

In Lincolnshire, the bat becomes a kibble. Other regional names are trevit, tribbitt, primstick or gelstick. Yet almost everywhere, the names of the implements give evidence of teutonic or old norse origins."

The height of the game's popularity came in the 1920s and 1930s when it was said that *"every other Yorkshireman was a leyker"*.

One of the advantages of the game was that in its purest form, it did not require much specialised equipment in order to play and most, if not all, could be made at home.

Although the most popular versions of the game have the knur being hit off a spell or a pin, another version sees the pot balanced on the head of the stick itself, flicked into the air and then hit as it returns to earth. This may be where the true origins come from.

Often referred to as "poor man's golf", knur and spell had a lot to offer in the cotton mill towns and mining areas affected by the depression of the 1930s as it took a lot of people to successfully run matches and kept many unemployed men occupied and out of trouble for much of the day.

There are essentially two versions of knur and spell – "*long knock*" and "*scoreplay*". Each is played in more or less the same way but in long knock, it is the furthest single hit of the day that wins. In score playing, each knock is measured with a chain 20 yards long (hence the old fashioned measurement of a chain…) and the player with the highest total score in yards over the course of the competition is declared the winner.

To give an idea of how popular the sport was at that time, there was a match at the Tempest Arms, Elslack, between Herbert Bateson and Tom Ellis.

It was a very big occasion and there were thousands of people and despite the absence of motorways and the fact that very few people had cars in those days, some even travelled from Halifax to watch.

The landlord of the pub took barrels of beer out to the field on a tractor and there were so many people in the pub that they had to open a barn. The landlord later said that the knur and spell men were the *"best customers he'd ever had in the pub. They would still be there at midnight!"*

Interestingly enough, there is hardly any mention of the game having been played by women. Evening Star journalist Terry Broadhurst wrote: *"It is rumoured that knur and spell was one of those marvellous excuses dreamed up by men to get away from the women and nearer to the beer!"*.

Alongside the prize money for any given contest, a knur and spell match would always attract lots of betting and this often helped to swell the crowds and fuel the excitement of the occasion.

Game Venues Near Colne

Popular venues for knur and spell included Tum Hills, overlooking the railway station where Jimmy Bullock was a train driver and Farmer Big Jack's field off Red Lane where the tippers had a hut to store their equipment to save them carrying it to the ground and back in the days before everyone had a car.

There was also Bannys big field at Foulridge, the Tempest estates at Elslack, and fields near the Emmott Arms and Hargeaves Arms at Laneshaw Bridge. The tippers also used Whittaker Farm but, as, Stuart says: *"My dad's cousin Tom Whittaker stopped us playing on his land. His excuse as that he was worried that his sheep would swallow the lost knurs!"*

Tales From The Forgotten World of Knur And Spell

Bert Walton swinging in Knur and Spell's 1930s heyday
Picture from "Kelbrook in Times Past" by Victor Laycock

Following pages:

In 1927, the Daily Mail carried a series by top cartoonist Tom Webster which attempted to explain the game of Knur and Spell, albeit in a rather tongue in cheek manner. By kind permission of the Daily Mail, the 3-part cartoon strip is reproduced here in its entirety.

COLNE GIANTS

Tales From The Forgotten World of Knur And Spell

MONDAY, The Daily Mail MARCH 14, 1927.

KNUR AND SPELL. By TOM WEBSTER.

STILL MANCHESTER.
SATURDAY.

GEORGE AND I HAVE WITNESSED A SAD SIGHT TO-DAY. WE HAVE SEEN A CHAMPION DETHRONED. UP TILL 4.30 P.M MARCH 12th 1927

MR EDON OF BARNSLEY WAS CHAMPION KNUR AND SPELL PLAYER OF THE WORLD

THEN A MR BULLOCK OF COLNE CAME ALONG AND DEPRIVED HIM OF HIS TITLE.

THE SETTING WAS DRAMATIC. OVER A STONE WALL TWO SHEEP LOOKED ON.

I MUST NOW TAKE THE LIBERTY OF EXPLAINING THE GAME OF KNUR AND SPELL BECAUSE I KNOW SO MANY PEOPLE IN THE WEST END OF LONDON WHO VERY RARELY PLAY IT.

IT CONSISTS OF HITTING A SMALL BALL (LIKE A LARGE MARBLE) AS FAR AS POSSIBLE. THEY GENERALLY PLAY THE BEST OF 25 "WALLOPS" AND THE LONGEST HIT WINS. THERE ARE TWO WAYS OF PLAYING IT. IN LANCASHIRE

THE BALL IS SUSPENDED FROM A SLING AND

THE PLAYER SIMPLY CLOUTS IT AS HARD AS HE CAN AND

THEN RUNS AFTER IT MUTTERING INCANTATIONS.

IN YORKSHIRE HOWEVER THEY PLAY IT FROM A KIND OF SPRING

THE BALL FLIES UP AT A TOUCH AND WITH THE CRY OF VIVE LA SHEFFIELD RINGING IN HIS EARS

THE PLAYER LETS FLY.

THE COSTUME IS THE SAME AS AT HURLINGHAM. CAP. BRACES. UNCREASED TROUSERS AND CLOGS WITHOUT SPATS.

BEFORE A MATCH STARTS ALL THE DAY IS TAKEN UP WITH ARGUING ABOUT WHICH PART OF THE GROUND THE TWO COMPETITORS SHALL USE.

AFTER EVERYTHING IS SETTLED THE PLAYERS THEN CALL IN THEIR COMMITTEE TO GET THEIR RESPECTIVE TEEING GROUNDS READY

AS FAR AS I COULD SEE THEY HAVE AN OFFICIAL SHOVELLER.

A MATHEMATICIAN AND

A GEOLOGIST—

AND NOW DEAR READER YOU HAVE NO IDEA HOW THE MATHEMATICIAN AND THE GEOLOGIST ARGUED

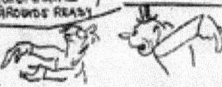

BUT WAIT UNTIL TUESDAY AND I WILL TELL YOU THE STORY OF THE MATCH.

COLNE GIANTS

Tales From The Forgotten World of Knur And Spell

MORE ABOUT KNUR AND SPELL. By TOM WEBSTER.

CONTINUING THE STORY OF THE GREAT KNUR AND SPELL MATCH.

IMMEDIATELY THE TWO MEN HAVE AGREED ABOUT CONDITIONS THE MATTER IS BY NO MEANS OVER. OH DEAR NO. GEORGE SAYS THAT AFTER A MATCH IS MADE THE KNUR AND SPELL PLAYER

SITS AND BROODS AT HOME.

AFTER A WHILE HE GETS TEMPERAMENTAL AND SENDS

FOR HIS TYPIST.

SAY — DEAR BILL. I'M KNUR AND SPELLING AGAIN AND I'LL MEET YOU NEXT THURSDAY.

LETTERS ARE THEN SENT OUT TO HIS STAFF. BECAUSE YOUR REAL KNUR AND SPELL PLAYER HAS TO HAVE

A MANAGER.

A CADDIE.

TWO OR THREE FRIENDS AND —

A MAN TO SEE THE GROUND IS LEVEL.

THE LATTER IS MOST IMPORTANT BECAUSE AFTER A MATCH IS MADE THIS MAN

HAS TO GO AROUND THE VENUE TO FIND

A REALLY NICE SPOT FOR THE GOVERNOR.

THE MOMENT A SUITABLE SITE IS FOUND —

THE KNUR AND SPELLER SENDS FOR HIS ARCHITECT —

AND THE MAN WHO CARRIES THE SPIRIT-LEVEL.

THE ENTIRE CAVALCADE THEN START FOR THE GROUND.

THIS STORY MUST STILL BE CONTINUED BECAUSE GEORGE SAYS THAT THERE IS A VERY THIN DEMARCATION LINE BETWEEN KNUR AND SPELL AND INSANITY.

[Daily Mail Copyright.]

AN EXACT SCIENCE. By TOM WEBSTER.

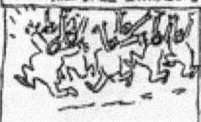

As mentioned in the cartoon, Joe Edon of Yorkshire and Bullock of Colne were big name players in their day. After Bullock, another Lancashire man, Crawshaw, won the unofficial "champion" tag and he was then beaten in the late 1930s by Colne's Billy Baxter.

Another top Lancashire player at that time was Tom Blackburn (pictured above) above in typical attire of the period, waistcoat, cap and clogs (clogs were still popular footwear in Lancashire in the 1930s). A tall man with broad shoulders, Blackburn was, like Baxter, the ideal build for a knur and spell player.

Tales From The Forgotten World of Knur And Spell

Tom Blackburn in action
(photos supplied by Neville Blackburn)

But for the intervention of the second world war, the game of knur and spell might well have remained a popular pastime among working folk. However, in the classless society that the servicemen came home to, much had changed. Priorities were different, rationing would still be in place for many years to come and the economy had to be rebuilt.

This resulted in the popularity of knur and spell plummeting in those post war years in Lancashire until the mid 1950s when a group of Colne based devotees came together to revive the game. These included Billy Baxter, Billy Southworth, Herbert Bateson and Ted Griffiths.

A player in the 1930s striking off a spell
(Source: Lancashire Library, Nelson Local Studies Collection)

Chapter 2: THE ART OF THE GAME

Although the actual game of knur and spell is quite straight forward, basically no more than hitting a small ball with a long stick, the game that developed in the 20th century became much more specialised. As such, people moved away from making their own equipment quite so much and certain experts became well known within the game.

In order to take part in a proper competition, any serious player needed:

- Sticks – normally around 4ft long but this could vary depending on the player's preference.
- Heads – these are precision made items and the hardness and quality is of great importance.
- Knurs - pot balls for hitting, often called "potties"
- Spell – a spring trap that launched the knur into the air. These were often made by the players themselves, which meant that designs often varied from player to player.
- Pin – a gallows like frame that was used in place of a spell. The knur was suspended on a wire from the top arm of the pin.

It was very important that the pin, or the spell, was on level ground so trowels of earth and spirit levels were often employed during the set up.

Furthermore the player would have heel pegs and side pegs that he placed in the ground to the side of his spell or pin to indicate his standing position. To ensure that they always stood in the same place in relation to the striking area, players would normally have a string line made to the right dimensions, which they would use to measure from the base edge of the spell or pin. The side pegs and heel pegs would thus be placed at the correct distance.

The match referee would also have his own special equipment:

- A whistle to sound at the start of the contest
- A set of numbered pegs to denote each player's hitting position
- A set of competition knurs with identification marks. The referee would take a note of the knur markings and the player using it to avoid cheating.
- Another set of pegs to mark their longest hit.
- A chain 20yards in length to use to measure the strike distance.

A draw was made to decide which player stood where and the order of play and the referee would stake out the striking positions, leaving a 5 yards gap between each player.

Although the players played as individuals in a match, it was necessary for them to have number of friends to help them. These were called "looker-outers" and they have to look out to see where the knur went once it had been hit. If the ground was damp, the flying knur would often sink into the ground on impact and be lost, so the role of the looker-outer was vital.

It was quite a specialised task and needed a lot of skill as the looker-outers only had a set time after the knur had been struck – say two or three minutes – to find the grounded knur or the shot would be called as "lost" and, thus, ruled ineligible.

Players drawing knurs at the start of a competition
(Source: Walter Ansell)

From where the player struck, a man (member of his group) stood behind the striker and he called to direct the people with the chain to measure the distance the knur had been hit.

The distance was always measured in a straight line from the player striking position to where the knur landed and the chain had to follow the contours of the ground. If that meant crossing a deep gully or a pond, then the chain had to be lowered down the sides of the obstacle, across the bottom and back up the other side to measure the full distance.

Large sums of money were often bet on knur and spell games, and there were often cases of skulduggery. A rival's looker-outer might stamp a good strike into the soft ground before anybody else saw it or remove a well placed peg before the final reckoning in order to give his own player an unfair advantage.

Also it was not unknown for people to tamper with another player's heel pegs to put him off his shot, so a team presence was vital to be a successful player.

Despite the apparent rough and ready nature of the game, the size and quality of a player's equipment was a decisive factor his playing performance and good heads were especially treasured.

Such was the kudos associated with a successful player that a top headmaker would often only make heads for one man and would refuse to let anyone else have them.

A man called Archie Robinson made heads in a workshop in Yorkshire. He was very proud of his workshop and was more than happy to show it off to visitors. However if anyone asked if they could buy some of the heads he would say: "*Oh no I don't sell heads to Lancashire lads*".

The basic rule was: the harder the head, the further the knur would travel and players would rub the heads with rosin to keep them supple. Players always took great care of their equipment.

Stuart says: *I used to hang my sticks up vertically in my loft over the winter months to keep them straight. And I kept my best heads rolled up in a wool sock to preserve them.*

In later years, when many of the old experts had faded from the scene, it became more important for the players themselves to be able to make their own equipment.

I made my own press for making heads and Barry Smith from Trawden - who was a joiner for the Council - we would shape heads that I had pressed. He was a very good player too and helped me make the heads very secure with dowels to prevent them flying off when I struck."

Tales From The Forgotten World of Knur And Spell

Spell or Pin?

The various regional differences in the game of knur and spell led to the strange situation whereby players from Lancashire used to hit off a pin while players from Yorkshire hit off a spell.

"Is it more sporting for a tipper to hit a potty in a pin than from a spell?" asked the Daily Mail in April 1970 as they reported the 1970 World Knur and Spell championship on top of the Pennines at Upper Greetland near Elland, Yorkshire.

The Yorkshire players accused the Lancashire competitors of making the game too easy by using a pin when they met and 1970 champion Eric Wilson from Sheffield said: *"anybody can hit a potty if it is still!"*

Colne's Ted Griffiths countered this by saying: *"The Yorkshiremen are always moaning. I admit it might be easier but they have an advantage because a knur hit from a spell usually travels further."*

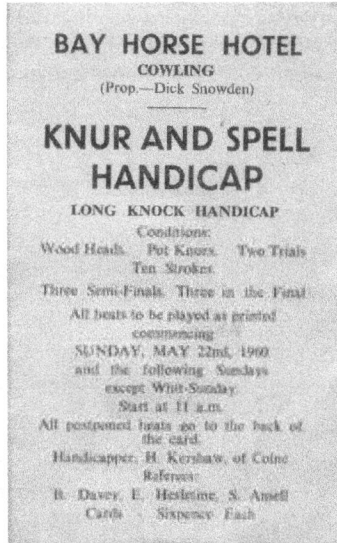

Posters for handicap events held around Colne in 1959 (left) and 1960 (right)
(Supplied by Stuart Greenfield)

Tales From The Forgotten World of Knur And Spell

THE HANDICAP EVENT

Organising a handicap was no mean feat as an event would run for a great many weeks. A heat involving 4 or 5 players would be played each weekend with each winner going through to the quarter-finals, semi finals and, eventually, the final itself.

With 10 heats, this meant that the player who won the first heat would have to wait at least 10 weeks – even more if later heats were put back due to bad weather – before playing in the next round.

To begin, the organiser would put a list up in the pub and all the people who wanted to play would have to put their names down.

The entrants would then be assessed by the "handicappers". These were the were the old experienced players and they would give each entrant a certain number of yards advantage depending on age, experience and past performances. Anybody that was an unknown quantity in the area had to play off "scratch", ie no advantage, in case he turned out to be very good…

This was very important as a great deal of money was placed on knur and spell games in side bets. Very often the betting men would earn a lot more money through gambling than the players themselves did from winning the event!

Many of the players –especially the older ones - were known by their nicknames, eg Irvine Bracewell was the *Dancing Master*, and there was also *Joiner Jack, Punch* etc.

At a contest, it was not unusual for these names rather than the players' own names to be written up on the board in the pub with the odds next to them.

As well as performance, the length of a player's stick was also taken into consideration for handicapping purposes. Players could use whatever length stick they liked but, as a longer stick tended to have a better "whip factor" and, theoretically at least, hit a shot further, the player with the longer stick would have to give a yard start to the other players for each inch they have over 4 feet long. Similarly for sticks shorter than 4 feet, a player was given a yard head start per inch for the same reason.

Tales From The Forgotten World of Knur And Spell

Stick	HEAT 1.	H'cap
3 6	W. Anness	12
3 6	H. Hartley	19
3 8	W. H. Southworth	61
3 6	E. Shepherd	12

Stick	HEAT 2.	
3 6	R. Bannister	15
3 6	E. Burkhill	19
3 8	W. Devonport	11
3 6	J. Laycock	39

Stick	HEAT 3.	
3 8	I. Bracewell	43
3 8	B. Smith	7
3 6	F. Whittaker	15
3 6	B. Sheader	15

Stick	HEAT 4.	
3 6	J. Lord	11
3 6	J. Hardacre	10
4 0	B. Rushton	14
3 8	A. Little	8

Stick	HEAT 5.	
3 8	S. Greenfield	4
3 8	W. Devonport	11
3 8	B. Smith	7
3 8	A. Little	8

Stick	HEAT 6.	H'cap
3 6	H. Hartley	19
3 6	L. Crabtree	15
3 6	J. Laycock	39
3 8	W. H. Southworth	61

Stick	HEAT 7.	
3 6	R. Bannister	15
3 6	L. Shuttleworth	11
4 0	H. Bateson	7
3 6	W. Greenfield	19

Stick	HEAT 8.	
3 6	H. Ombler	19
3 6	J. Hardacre	10
3 6	E. Burkhill	19
3 6	H. Cardwell	19

Stick	HEAT 9.	
3 6	F. Whittaker	15
3 6	L. Shuttleworth	11
3 6	E. Shepherd	12
3 6	F. Binns	15
3 6	E. Dawson	10

Stick	HEAT 10.	
3 6	N. Gamson	15
3 6	H. Cardwell	19
4 0	B. Rushton	14
4 0	J. Travis	14
4 0	H. Bateson	7

A Typical Handicap Book From 1959
Source: Herbert Bateson

At the time of the revival in the 1950s, the older players were keen to attract young blood into the sport so the newcomers to the game – known as novices - were given a very generous 17 yards start.

In the same way that novices were given a head start to give them a reasonable chance against the top players, older players who were past their prime were also given a head start to allow them to take an active part as well. This often led to the playing veterans being given 40 or 50 yards advantage over the top players of the day.

Stuart recalls: "*A farmer called Ramsden Smith used to use a really long "whippy" stick, which went right round his body and knocked him off balance when he swung. I remember seeing him fall over after he had struck and roll down the hill but he bounced back on to his feet. He was very fit, even into his later years.*"

Setting Up
(or "*Pricking In*")

Stuart explains:

"*To set up the playing area you used to level the ground with a shovel and ashes. I used a stick with a ring marked round it on which I marked the height of my shot.*"

Setting Up The Pin

Top: Setting the pin vertically using the plumb line.

Middle: Checking the level of the horizontal bar,

Bottom: Placing the knur in the loop of thread

(Photo sources: John Marshall, West Riding News Service & Stuart Greenfield)

Tales From The Forgotten World of Knur And Spell

The Swing
Stuart demonstrates the swing watched by Herbert Bateson, Fred Ansell and Leonard Kershaw (Photo source: Stuart Greenfield)

"I never used to look when I was swinging. I'd put a pin down and had some string in a triangle with a hook in one angle. This was stretched out and kept straight with a piece of wood to mark the standing area to measure where the feet would go. A spirit level and a plumb line were also used. Though these were more for show than anything else, the plumb line was quite important."

The Problem With Knurs

Early knurs were made of wood or lignum vitae with carved surfaces. They were painted white to make them easier to spot in the grass and this made them look similar to a modern day golf ball. Latterly they were made of smooth pot ½ oz in weight, rather like a marble.

Interestingly enough, the game of knur and spell almost died out after the second world war because the pottery industry found a way to reduce waste.

Before the war, surplus bits of clay were made into hard little balls of pot and poorly paid pottery workers made extra money selling them to players for use as knurs. Then a new process was introduced which gathered up all the waste clay for re-using. Knurs all but disappeared and this undoubtedly contributed to the decline in the game.

Then, in 1981, a small pottery in Ivegate, Colne, offered to try and help make knurs.

The process was very difficult because the balls had to weigh ½ oz exactly when they were finished and they had to be hand rolled, fired and glazed to very specific parameters, which was only arrived at by trial and error.

Chapter 3: THE PERSONALITIES

Stuart Greenfield
Official World Champion
1971 and 1973

I played my first long knock handicap at Laneshaw Bridge in 1957 and novices like myself received 13 yards head start based on 4 foot sticks.

I considered this to be too generous, but the handicappers were trying to encourage new players into the game at that time and were quite successful in this.

My longest knock measured in a handicap was 12 score 12 yds 2'3", ie 252 yds 2 foot 3 inches for which I received a £1 prize. Bill Baxter told me that he had never sent a knur as far, although I still consider him a better long knock player than myself.

I was behind in my heat with two strokes to go and then my dad suggested I try a larger head. I did so and just managed to win through. I then had to keep practicing on my own for the following 14 weeks to stay sharp for the final

Playing against me in the final were three well known tipping personalities – Jimmy Laycock, Billy Anness from Laneshaw Bridge and Irvine Bracewell. I played off a 3'8" stick receiving 17yds start, Jimmy Laycock played off 3'6" with 50yds, Irvine Bracewell played off 3'8" with 50yds and Billy Anness off 3'6" with 13yds.

After my first strike, Billy Lee - a local sporting personality - raised a £10 note in the air and shouted that he thought that it would be the winning shot, challenging anyone who disagreed to match his £10 bet. This sort of impromptu betting happened quite often at knur and spell games but nobody took him up and I won the match with my first hit.

Emmott Arms Handicap Final - March 1958
(source: Stuart Greenfield)

Nearly everybody on this photo is a player or keen follower of knur and spell. Below are mentioned but a few of the main characters.

John Travis (5th left), Bert Walton (8th left), Billy Anness (13th left), Irvine Bracewell (18th left –holding stick, no cap), Herbert Bateson (20th left head in background), Sam Ansell (22nd left, in coat and scarf), Jimmy Laycock (centre front with black jacket), Billy Bolton (centre back with bare head), Billy Greenfield (centre front with coat and scarf), Derek Wilson (19th right, middle row in cap and scarf), Stuart Greenfield (in front at pin), Billy Southworth (9th right, at front with hat and glasses), Joe Emerson (6th right), Reuben Bannister (5th right), Harry Kershaw, (4th right at back), Billy Green (2nd right), Billy Baxter (far right)

Leonard Kershaw
Official World Champion 1972 and since 1991

Len Kershaw is a man of many talents. Apart from being the reigning world knur and spell champion, he has played football, cricket, bowls and swimming, he is a scratch player at snooker and sings with the Colne Glee Choir and the Operatic Society.

He keeps greyhounds and would think nothing of walking with them to see a knur and spell match at Elslack – a good 9 mile round trip – and looking out for a game along the way.

Stuart Says:

Len is very enthusiastic in everything he takes part in and he is very competitive. Even when he was working as traffic warden, he made sure that he gave out more tickets than anyone else!

I certainly think that playing with Leonard improved my game as it fired me up more. If it had just been left up to me I probably wouldn't have pushed myself so hard and had the success that I did.

Len was another of the young players who was drawn into the game upon its revival in the 1950s. He once won a handicap (Duttons Brewery) and the head flew off and went nearly as far as his knur!

Len Kershaw being presented with the Duttons Brewery Cup at the Emmott Arms, Laneshaw Bridge, September 1958

Stuart Greenfield (far left), Ted Griffiths (2nd left), Harry Kershaw (3rd left at back), Billy Baxter (4th left), Micky Little (7th left, behind prizegiver), Billy Anness (front centre behind cup), Len Kershaw (front right of centre), Fred Hargreaves (4th right behind Kershaw), Billy Southworth (2nd right front), Herbert Bateson (far right front).

Sam Ansell

A clogger by trade, Sam Ansell was a real celebrity in Colne.

He was an outstanding amateur sportsman who, in his prime, had been a wrestling corner second, champion ice skater, and later worked as a swimming pool attendant

His real name was actually Walter but Ansell wanted to choose a nickname for himself that sounded more sporty.

Funnily enough, his inspiration came for the jersey that he always wore when he was ice skating. On the front it had emblazoned "Skating Association of Montreal" and that is show he came up with the name of SAM.

He didn't really have any background himself in knur and spell but when the group of Colne enthusiasts revived the game in the 1950s he offered to be the referee and got the job as he was the only one that offered!

On one of his first officiating occasions, not really knowing how the game was played, Ansell stood too close to the players and was knocked out by a player's swing!

Sam was always a very dapper dresser and his flamboyant apparel was the source of much mirth among the players. One time they were travelling to match and passed a field where a travelling circus had pitched their tent and somebody suggested that he ought to join them as a clown.

It is said that, while serving in the RAF during the war, Ansell met a very youthful Jimmy Young and persuaded him to take up singing. However, the Radio 2 DJ does not recall this.

Stuart says: *"Sam Ansell and Herbert Bateson were once invited to appear on Granada TV in Manchester to explain the art of knur and spell.*

They both arrived wearing Lancashire clogs with wooden soles and heavy irons that Sam had made in his shop for the occasion!

After showing off their sticks and heads, they were asked "what are these on your feet" to which Herbert replied "clogs – part of the tippers equipment". After receiving their fee from Granada they retired to the nearest public house."

Sam Ansell skating in 1932
(source: Geoff Crambie)

Billy Baxter

Billy Baxter from Colne was the world champion from 1937 to 1969. He took the title from Jim Crawshaw, a farmer from the Sheffield area. The match took place at the Alma Tipping Ground at Laneshaw Bridge in front of a record crowd.

In times gone by, local cricket matches also drew large crowds. On the same day as this game, there was also a Colne v Nelson derby match where Ama Singh and Learie Constantine were the respective pros.

There were so many spectators that the cricket ground overflowed and people were sitting on the walls, even though it cost 6d. to get in.

However the knur and spell match between Baxter and Crawshaw just up the road attracted an even bigger crowd than the cricket match, such was local enthusiasm for the game.

The outcome was that Baxter won over 25 rises but Crawshaw said that he "wasn't satisfied and wanted a return match...". He was a farmer and insisted that the return match be held on his own ground near Sheffield. This was duly arranged but Baxter won again.

Stuart says: *"Billy Baxter was the finest player I have ever seen. I have met Jimmy Bullock who many good judges said was better than Baxter. He was a Colne train driver and had an army of backers and supporters. They often travelled to Yorkshire and beat the local champions there, one of which was the legendary Joe Edon, who was never known to turn down a challenge."*

Billy Southworth

Stuart says: *A life long supporter of knur and spell and a very good friend. He followed me all over Yorkshire looking out for my knurs.*

Ted Griffiths
"The Colne Giant"

Standing 6'2", Colne civil servant Ted Griffiths was known as the "Colne Giant".

He was one of the enthusiasts who helped revive the game in Colne in the 1950s and he claimed to have remained undefeated in at least a dozen challenge matches but he never won a handicap event.

During the run up to the 1970 world championships, many people tipped him to win the title and the TV coverage prior to the event focused on his tall stature.

They even filmed him stepping over walls and fences with a camera positioned close to the ground to make him look even more of a "giant"!

Griffiths had a bit of a reputation for telling tall stories about knur and spell exploits and everybody knew that what he said was rather tongue in cheek.

However one day, Herbert Bateson got fed up with his exaggerations and famously said to Griffiths:

"You're all right up to 'ere Ted, (indicating his neck!). *but the rest's wood."*

Whenever a pub hosted a knur and spell event, they laid on hospitality for the players and officials. Being a "big lad", Ted Griffiths was renowned for his healthy appetite on such occasions and was jokingly known as the "world champion pork pie eater..."

Ted Griffiths striking in a handicap competition at the Hargreaves Arms, Laneshaw Bridge

Also playing are Tommy Mason, Eugene Dawson, Wallace Devonport and Tommy Hartley. (Source: Ron Ansell)

Fred "Snacky" Hargreaves

Fred Hargreaves from Trawden was the score-playing champion for a long period, having won the title from Joiner Jack from Todmorden.

A big crowd of family and friends travelled to support him that day and there were tears of joy as it was such a great achievement.

Not only did he beat Joiner Jack, who had himself been the score-playing champion for many years and had an awesome reputation but to win on his home turf in Yorkshire!

Snacky also had a big reputation as a dog breeder, breeding champion English setters that he showed all over the country.

Stuart says: "*I never saw him miss a knur at long knock even though he was the score playing champion.*"

Tales From The Forgotten World of Knur And Spell

Jimmy Laycock
"Apple Chops"

Jimmy was the local postman and delivered mail on a GPO bike. He was also a champion pigeon flyer. His idols were Joe Edon and Bill Baxter and he would travel for miles to watch a top knur and spell match.

Stuart says: "*There was a time when knurs became very difficult to get hold of but everybody knew that Applechops had a good supply, although he refused to share them around with his mates."*

It was well known that he kept his knur and spell tackle under his bed for safe keeping and, at that time, he had a lady friend with whom he often went for a drink at the Red Lion pub in Colne. After a lot of cajoling and much plying with drinks, she was eventually persuaded, to try and obtain some of Applechops' precious knurs and sell them to some of the other members of the gang."

At first, he was quite pleased to see that his friends had found a new source of knurs and stopped trying to cadge his but was rather annoyed once he found out where they were really coming from!"

John Travis

Stuart says: *Colne clogger, a good head maker and top player. I bought my pin and some sticks and heads from his father, Old Travis, when I first started playing.*

Old Travis was a skilled cabinet maker and the gear I bought from him was real quality.

Harry Kershaw

Harry Kershaw was Leonard's father and also the bookmaker.

He got involved with knur and spell because someone was needed to help with the handicap odds and his expertise in the field made him the natural choice.

Stuart says: *Some people called him Harry Shortodds. He was a regular at tipping matches and I found him very fair.*

He became the general secretary of the weavers union.

In the run up to my first handicap final, I'd heard that there was a lot of money being bet on me to win. I was wanting to get engaged to my girlfriend at the time but needed money to buy a ring.

So I told her she'd have to wait and see if I won, which she wasn't too pleased about – her future happiness depending on the swing of a stick..!.

I went to see Harry Kershaw and told him I'd like to put a bet on myself to win the final but by that time, there was already a lot of money riding on me. He was worried that he might end up out of pocket and said that I couldn't place my own bet.

I was a bit annoyed about this because everyone else looked set to make a lot of money out of me winning and I was going to miss out. So I told him, if I can't place a bet, then I won't play!

Faced with the even worse scenario of me pulling out and having to give back all the stake money, Harry agreed to let me bet on the semi final instead and have a percentage of my dad's bet on the final.

Billy Anness

Billy Anness (father of Jimmy Anness) was a slight man but Billy Baxter always described him as *"pound for pound he was one of the best players ever seen".*

Stuart says: *"Billy made some of the best heads in Lancashire including 2 from birds eye maple that I used to win the world championships and 1 that won the Spring Rock Cup made of sycamore."*

One time a young novice player called Sam Spencer tried to buy some heads from Billy, but he refused, saying that he "only made heads for Len Kershaw!!"

His nephew Jimmy Tillotson once complained that Billy was his own uncle and wouldn't even sell any heads to him either..."

Herbert Bateson

Stuart says: "A top class player. He helped me in matches and gave me good advice. He knew more about the game than anyone I've met. He gave me most of his best heads and sticks. He once said to me "don't forget tha's got to tec thirty bob into Yorkshire to come back with a pound..!" and I knew exactly what he meant. If I didn't train hard, I would not win anything in Yorkshire. I never forgot his advice."

Ironically he had been born and bred in Yorkshire himself at Kelbrook, so he must have known what he was talking about."

The last time I saw Herbert on a tipping ground was when he came to support me in a competition at the Hargreaves Arms, even though he was very ill and frail by then. They covered the match on Radio 5 and interviewed Herbert afterwards."

When he died he was cremated at Skipton in Yorkshire and the funeral cortège took a route past his favourite tipping grounds."

Bert Walton

Stuart says: An outstanding score-player, second only to Snacky Hargreaves. He nearly always reached the semis or finals of long knock handicaps.

Once when I played against him, he knocked clean out of the field and they had to find a bigger field to play on!"

I gave him 45yds start at the Hare and Hounds final at Foulridge and beat him. Most people, including myself, thought it impossible. It was supposed to have been his swansong and I spoilt the party. Baxter said it was my best ever performance but Walton never spoke to me again..."

Irvine Bracewell
"The Dancing Master"

Bracewell was a single man with a flair for dancing and was often to be found on the dance floor at the Ambulance Hall. This was quite a contrast to the rough and ready types that knur and spell usually attracted and made him very popular with the ladies, hence his acquired nickname.

YORKSHIRE PLAYERS

The game of knur and spell was more widely played in Yorkshire than in Lancashire and still survives today in certain areas. Here are but a few of the main names from the period that this book covers.

Frank Lenthall - "Big Yank"

1979 world champion and winner of the revival handicap at the Hargreaves Arms in 1995.

Stuart says: *Frank was the player we feared the most. By far the best player I have seen using a spell, he nearly always hit 10 out of 10. His father trained him. He had been a friend of the legendary Joe Edon and they also trained sporting dogs together.*

Eric Wilson
First "official" world
champion in 1970.

Tom Chambers
Yorkshire favourite

Fred Trueman
ex Yorkshire &
England cricketer

Stuart says: *"Fred Trueman was very supportive of the game of knur and spell and a good player in his own right. Many people thought he would have won the 1971 world championship but they couldn't find his knur."*

Tales From The Forgotten World of Knur And Spell

HANDICAP SEMI FINAL AT ELSLACK

Ronnie Bolton (2nd left front), Billy Southworth (centre front), Tony Bailiff (2nd right front), Sam Ansell (far right front), Stuart Greenfield (2nd left back), Len Shuttleworth (middle, no tie), Billy Bolton (centre rear with black jacket), William Greenfield (3rd right back), Fred Ansell Sam's brother (2nd right back)

TEMPEST ARMS, ELSLACK

Herbert Bateson (far left kneeling), Fred Hargreaves (4th left standing in cap), Reubin Bannister (7th left standing), Long Dick Hartley (centre left standing in hat), Billy Bolton (centre standing no hat), Micky Little (9th right standing), Sam Ansell (8th right), Wallace Devonport (3rd right), Irvine Bracewell (2nd right), Stuart Greenfield (far right)

Stuart says: "*Ready to strike off in a £5- a side match with Bill Baxter and Herbert Bateson. I had smashed my best head a few weeks before playing the Colne giant Ted Griffitths in a much more serious match for an undisclosed side stake.*"

Chapter 4: THE WORLD CHAMPIONSHIPS

As mentioned earlier, the game of knur and spell had a rich history of champions stretching back into the 19th century. However, because of the fragmentation of the sport after the second world war, large scale gatherings became very rare.

The result of this was that Colne's Billy Baxter remained the reigning unofficial world champion for over 30 years by virtue of the title that he had won before the war.

Then in 1970, once the game of knur and spell had become more popular again, the first official "world" championship was played, under the sponsorship of Gannex raincoats who put up a cup and prize money.

Billy Baxter
(Source: Yorkshire Post)

However, in common with the American "world series" at baseball, the knur and spell playing world did not actually extend very far.

In fact, all the competitors came from the West Riding of Yorkshire and the town of Colne in Lancashire but Lancashire personality and knur and spell referee Sam Ansell explained why it was still called "world championship":

"It's because we are the only ones who know how to play it properly. It's a game that's gone on around here for donkeys years but myself and a group of others revived the sport on a group basis about 12 years ago. There were unofficial world championships before but in 1970 it was made official with prize money and a cup."

The Colne based firm of Melfar, which had some association with Gannex, was invited to provide a team of four people to represent Lancashire at the event. The team manager selected Ted Griffiths, Len Kershaw, Billy Baxter and Herbert Bateson.

Billy Baxter said that said that it was a shame as Greenfield was a much better player than he by that stage and that Stuart should play instead of him. However the manager said there was quite a bit of money (bets) already being placed so Stuart said he would not go because it would look a bit dubious.

Baxter then offered to say that he was ill on the day of the game and drop out at the last minute so that Stuart could play instead. But Stuart decided that, if he wasn't going to play in his own right, he didn't want to play at all so he didn't even travel to watch the match.

So first ever "official" world championship for knur and spell was held over Easter weekend of 1970 but, despite the strong Lancashire showing, the winner was Sheffield's Eric Wilson who won with a 197yds strike

Having missed out on the 1970 world championship Stuart was even more determined to be invited to the 1971 event.

He entered a handicap at a pub in Barnsley where he hoped to come up against Eric Wilson. He had previously sent him a letter challenging him to a match, hoping to beat him and thus get into the championship by that route.

However, Wilson did not play and it was long hard day. Stuart only managed second place behind a man called Smedley, who was the best player among the group from Sheffield that day.

Much to Stuart's annoyance, the same four players were invited to play in the 1971 World Championship.

However, one evening during a conversation in at the Colne British Legion Club with Ted Griffiths, the Giant suggested that, if Stuart wanted to take part, then he should write to the brewery who had taken over sponsoring the event – Websters.

They got the address from a label on a bottle of beer and Stuart wrote off telling of his outstanding record in handicaps and challenge matches.

He received a reply from Websters saying that they were only sponsoring the event and had no direct input on the actual organisation of it but that they would pass it on.

Then Stuart got a telephone call from Barry Cockcroft, the Yorkshire TV producer who was making a film of the day's events, who said that he'd meet him on the morning of the match and make sure he played - which he duly did!

Fred Trueman ready to strike
Source: Daily Mail

Easter Tuesday 1971

Stuart recalls: *"Being very much a Yorkshire thing, the event hadn't had that much publicity over our side of the Pennines. I was driving myself over into Yorkshire and as I got nearer to the venue, I couldn't believe my eyes. There were AA signs pointing the way and crowds of people all over the place."*

The added interest of the TV coverage and the presence of the celebrities had made this year's event much bigger than the previous year's with some 20 tippers chasing the £200 prize.

Among the opposition waiting for the Lancashire quintet were reigning champion Eric Wilson and his two brothers, Robert and Roy and Stanley Edon, son of Jospeh Edon who had been English champion for some 25 years in the 1920s and 30s.

Tales From The Forgotten World of Knur And Spell

Former Yorkshire and England cricket player Fred Trueman took part and Geoff Boycott, the Yorkshire batsman, was also there but had returned from cricket tour of south east Asia with an injured shoulder and could not play.

Stuart recalls: *"Another of the competitors was a professional tennis player – a giant of a man from Cowling in Yorkshire called Tony Winstanley. He arrived on the field wearing a leopard skin coat and Austin Mitchell, commentating for Yorkshire Television, said that when the men from Colne saw him, they were shaking in their shoes!"*

Because of the large number of people playing, the match was played over 5 rises each, rather than the 20 or 25 that would normally be the case in a big game.

Stuart says: *"It meant that there was a long time to wait in between strikes. Many of the players spent the time drinking and soaking up the lively atmosphere. I wasn't really into all that stuff so I just went and sat in my car with my hat and scarf on, waiting for my next strike. That enabled me to stay focused on my own game and it paid off in the end."*

Striking 18th out of 20, Stuart won the match with a knock of 225 yards. Len Kershaw was standing in the heather when a knur dropped at his feet. It was hard to find the knurs in the heather, so this was a lucky shot.

Stuart, unaware of how far his shot had actually gone was halfway across the field, trying to catch sight of it when he met Billy Baxter – well the worse for drink by that stage - who was rushing the other way. He ran over to Stuart, saying that no-one would beat that shot, flung his arms round him and they both fell to the ground, rolling about. Stuart had won.

Freddy Trueman presented him with the winner's cheque and said *"you chaps are the salt of the earth"*.

Tales From The Forgotten World of Knur And Spell

Stuart Greenfield
1971 World Champion
(Source: Evening Star)

**1972 World Champion
Len Kershaw
with daughter Millie**
*(Source: West Riding
News Service)*

1972

The 1972 World championship was held at the Spring Rock, near Halifax and, once again, a strong Lancashire contingent took part.

Despite fierce opposition from the local Yorkshire players, the world title headed back to Lancashire for the second time in a row as Leonard Kershaw won with a 200 yard strike.

He recalls: *"There was strong wind that day and it was toppling the knurs (making them drop sharply and lose height and distance). The other players kept whacking their shots as hard as they could but I turned my head down so that the angle was lower. Instead of flying up and getting caught by the wind, my knurs stayed low and just flew over the brow of the hill."*

1973

The 1973 World Championship was played at the Dodsworth Colliery Sports Ground in October. Yorkshire TV once again filmed the event with Austin Mitchell behind the microphone and Fiery Fred Trueman was there to give his patronage.

Stuart Greenfield won the world title for a second time with a 171 yd strike while reigning champion Kershaw – the second of only 3 Lancashire players in the match - came second with 158 yards. Barnsley's Thomas Chambers came third.

Sam Ansell was the match referee. Afterwards he said: *"the wind was against all the players and so many of the strikes were not as long as last year. Stuart's efforts, however, are still very commendable in the circumstances and he fully deserves to win the trophy."*

The Yorkshire players were very keen to win the competition but in the end Stuart ran out a convincing winner. The Yorkshire men were very disappointed."

Indeed, this was a great disappointment to the local spectators who had fully expected to see a Yorkshire victory.

In fact, after the match, things began to get a little boisterous as the flow of Yorkshire bitter continued unabated. A few men decided to climb up the support poles of the refreshments marquee. At this point, the police were called to calm the men down but they only managed to succeed in annoying the onlookers who had already placed bets on who would win the climbing competition.

Kershaw, Greenfield & Chambers, 1973
Source: West Riding News Service

Many in the crowd were Yorkshire miners and there was still some animosity towards the police following the recent miners' strike. The whole thing flared up into a massive brawl and Websters decided that they didn't want to sponsor the event again as it had given them too much bad publicity.

Not one to bask in the limelight, or indeed confrontation, newly crowned champion Stuart Greenfield sloped off and was sitting quietly in the pub when the telephone rang. Everybody else's was so caught up with the hullabaloo that was going on outside that he had to go and answer it himself.

It turned out to be the Yorkshire Post ringing up to find out how the match had gone and to see if Tommy Chambers had won!

June 1979

After the débacle with the miners at the 1973 event, Websters Brewery withdrew their patronage for several years and the world championship was not played for again until 1979.

By now, the old wounds had healed a little and the Yorkshire brewers were once again tempted back into the fold.

The event took place at the Red Lion pub at Stainland near Halifax and Stuart Greenfield was there to defend his crown, along with Len Kershaw, in front of some 500 spectators with £500 prize money at stake.

Frank Lenthall

Challengers that day included Tommy Chambers, Selwyn Schofield - a larger than life pensioner from Greetland and number 1 tipper in the area, 70 year old George Ellis who was said to roar like a bull when he hit a good potty (Tom Ellis – George's brother – was a joiner and made heads that were, by all accounts, bettered only by those from Archie Robinson).

Because of a shortage of potties Greenfield and Kershaw had to practice with marbles and an appeal went out before the championship for any former players to come forward and donate them.

This time, history was made and, for the first time since before the second world war, the knur and spell title headed east of the Pennines back to Yorkshire after a 210 yard shot handed victory to Frank Lenthall of Barnsley, known as Big Yank.

Lenthall told the Yorkshire Post: "*I just dropped lucky, I've only been out of the top 4 once and I've been playing since 1969*".

Len Kershaw came second, Stuart Greenfield, defending champion, third and Eric Wilson 4th.

Tales From The Forgotten World of Knur And Spell

Stuart Greenfield striking at the 1979 event
Source: Yorkshire Post

Billy Baxter, who had been the unofficial world champion from 1937 to 1957 was a "looker outer" at this game for Stuart at this game even though he was now in his 70s.

Commenting on the disappointing crowds by 1930s standards, he said: "*when I was in my pomp in Lancashire, there were many a thousand competitors around. In the old days when chaps like Joe Eden of Barnsley, Jimmy Bullock of Colne and Crawshaw of Sheffield, there were five or six thousand turned up to watch.*"

1991

In May 1991, the ancient game was revived once again as Websters brewery sponsored an invitation world championship for the Websters Pennine Cup

The match took place at the Bradshaw Tavern, Halifax and was contested by 3 players from Lancashire and 3 from Yorkshire.

Channel 4 cameras filming the event
(Source: John Marshall Photography)

The action was filmed by Channel 4's for Transworld Sport programme and this time it was a Lancashire 1-2-3 as Len Kershaw came first with a knock of 175 yards, Stuart Greenfield second (170yds) and Ted Griffiths third (165 yds).

Stuart says: "*That was to be the last time that the official world championship was ever played for and Len Kershaw holds the Pennine Cup trophy to this day.*"

Len Kershaw – 1991 World Champion
(Source: John Marshall Photography)

The top knur and spell players - 1991
Left to right: Ted Griffiths, Percy Sugden, Frank Lenthall, ?, Stuart Greenfield, Len Kershaw
(source: John Marshall Photography)

This picture, taken at the last world championship event is good demonstration of why knur and spell died out as a universal competitive sport. The self same players who were at the top of the game in the 1950s and 1960s were still the top players in the 1990s and little or no young blood had come through to take over.

Stuart says: "*I remember the last handicap that I took part in. It was at the Hare and Hounds at Black Lane Ends and a Colne Times reporter came to report on the game.*

The other players were all late turning up. They didn't take it anywhere near as seriously by then and the reporter said "I'm running later now – I've got more important things to do than wait for this.

I turned to him and replied "NOTHING is more important that knur and spell..!" but, sadly, those days seem to have gone."

1995

As time went by, interest in knur and spell dwindled in Colne. One reason was the lack of suitable fields within easy reach, Another was, with so many other activities on offer, young people were reluctant to take up the sport. However, not far from the original "tipping grounds" of the earlier generations of Colne "lakers", the Hargreaves Arms pub at Laneshaw Bridge organised a few long knock competitions in the early 1990s.

The 1995 event was recorded by BBC Radio 5 but, despite being played on Lancashire soil, it was Yorkshire's day. Frank Lenthall won with Stuart Greenfield second. Third and fourth places also went to players from Yorkshire.

Tel. Editorial/other departments Nelson 612561, Classified Burnley 422331.

News

▲ LONG-KNOCK: The traditional game of knur and spell is peculiar to the Lancashire-Yorkshire border, so where better to have a competition than the Hargreaves Arms, Laneshaw Bridge? Photo: Anthony Braithwaite

▲ DAVID BELL

YOU CAN'T KNOCK IT

Old Colne sport makes come-back

DEVOTEES of the ancient game knur and spell descended on the Hargreaves Arms, Laneshaw Bridge, on Saturday, for a long-knock competition.

The local pub hosted a similar event only two years ago, and landlord Mr David Bell was delighted that his pub had been picked once more.

Knur and spell is a traditional game which originated on the Lancashire-Yorkshire border, and it involves hitting a ball with an implement similar to a golf stick. Whoever whacks the ball furthest wins.

A Radio 4 production team were at the Hargreaves Arms on Saturday to record the tig day, and a feature on knur and spell will go out in July.

The winner of the long-knock was Big Yank from Barnsley, and the runner-up was Stewart Greenfield, of Colne. Third place went to Nigel Flowers of Stainross, and fourth place went to Steve Morgan of Sutton and Craven.

The long-knock started at 2 p.m. and the referee was Mr Leonard Dewhurst.

Mr Bell said: "They are trying to revive the game at the moment.

"The players equipment is hand-made and there is a lot more to the game of knur and spell than meets the eye."

Unfortunately, that was to be the swansong for the game of knur and spell, at least as far as serious participation in Lancashire was concerned. Specialised interest groups in areas of Yorkshire have kept the sport alive to a certain extent but the old diehards from Colne have now all hung up their sticks and heads and retired.

More recent attempts to demonstrate the game at country fairs in a bid to woo new younger players have met with little success and knur and spell – a game which once attracted crowds of thousands and hundreds of pounds in betting – is now little more then an old curiosity to the modern population.

Tales From The Forgotten World of Knur And Spell

3 Colne Giants
Ted Griffiths (left) Stuart Greenfield (right) Len Kershaw (at pin)

If you have enjoyed this book, you might also like to read about more 20th century Lancashire history in "Darwen Football Club Memories" and "Blackpool To Bond Street!"

ISBN-13: 978-0953978243

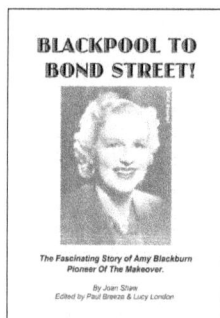

ISBN-13: 978-0953978250

Both available from www.poshupnorth.com, Amazon, Kindle, and all other quality outlets...!

FEMALE POETS – VOLUME 1
ISBN 978-1-909643-02-4
126 pages paperback

FEMALE POETS - VOLUME 2
ISBN 978-1-909643-17-8
186 pages paperback

No Woman's Land
ISBN 978-1-909643-07-9
128 pages paperback

The Somme 1916
ISBN 978-1-909643-24-6
136 pages paperback

Arras, Messines, Passchendaele &
More   ISBN: 978-1-909643-21-5 -
150 Pages Paperback

Women Casualties – Vol1
ISBN 978-1-909643-26-0
86 pages paperback

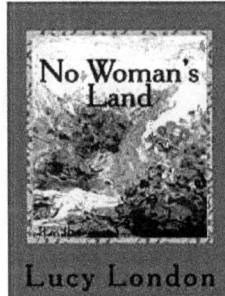

Aviator Poets & Writers of WW1
ISBN: 978-1-909643-22-2
66 pages paperback with photos

Poets' Corners In Foreign Fields
ISBN 978-1-909643-08-6
72 pages paperback with photos

Guns & Pencils
ISBN 978-0-953978-22-9
36 pages paperback

Tales From The Forgotten World of Knur And Spell

https://worldofnadjamalacrida.blogspot.com

www.poshupnorth.com

www.inspirationalwomenofww1.blogspot.co.uk

Tales From The Forgotten World of Knur And Spell

www.pendlewarpoetrycompetition.blogspot.com

The world's biggest
Free to Enter
poetry competition.

Entries close 30th
September each year.

For past results, rules and
details of how to enter visit
the website.

Previous anthologies available by mail order:

www.ingramcontent.com/pod-product-compliance
Lightning Source LLC
Chambersburg PA
CBHW060041040426
42331CB00032B/2031